JEFF CASE PAINTINGS 2010 - 2020

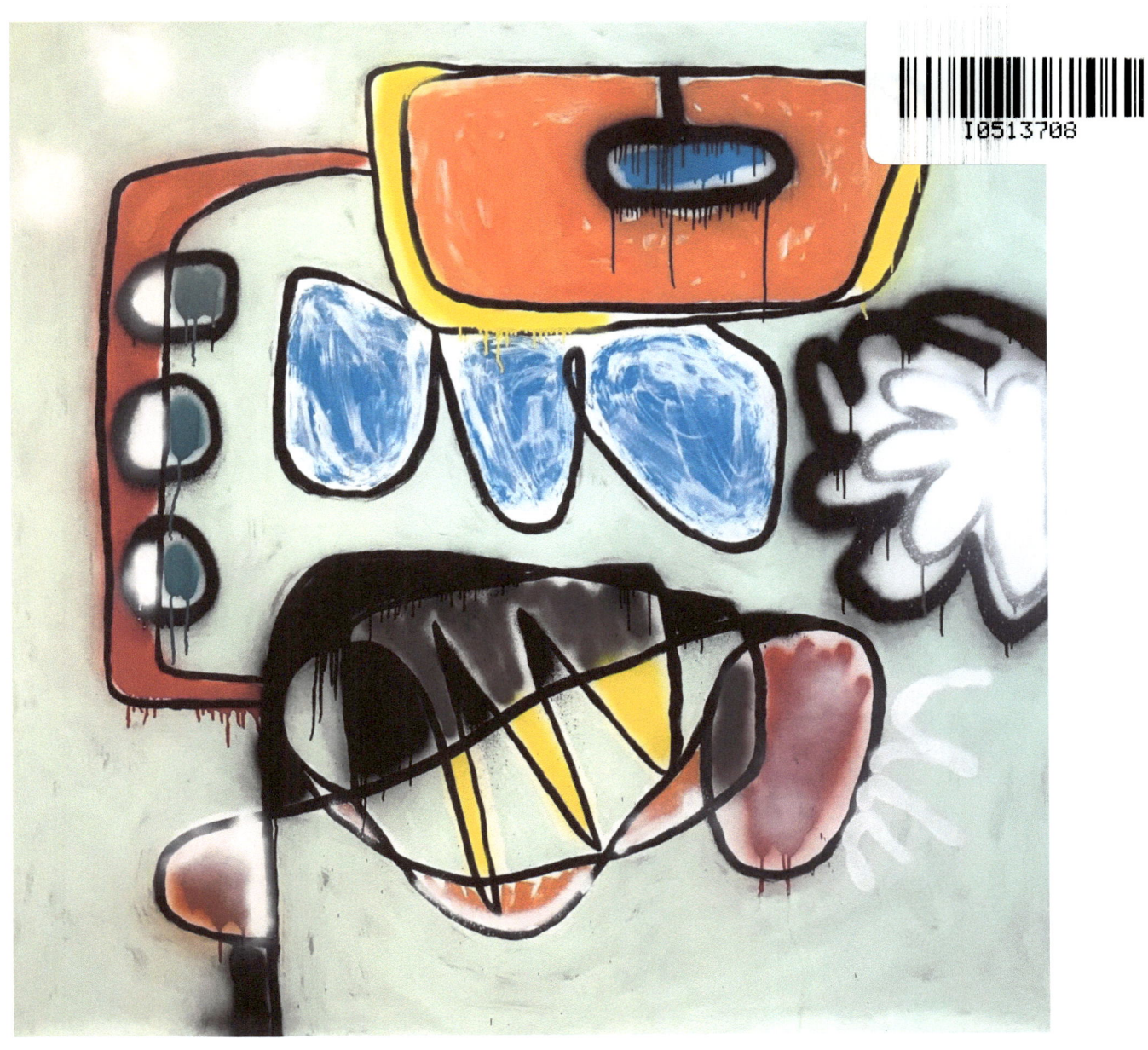

Jeff Case

Paintings 2010 - 2020

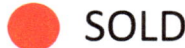 SOLD

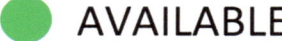 AVAILABLE

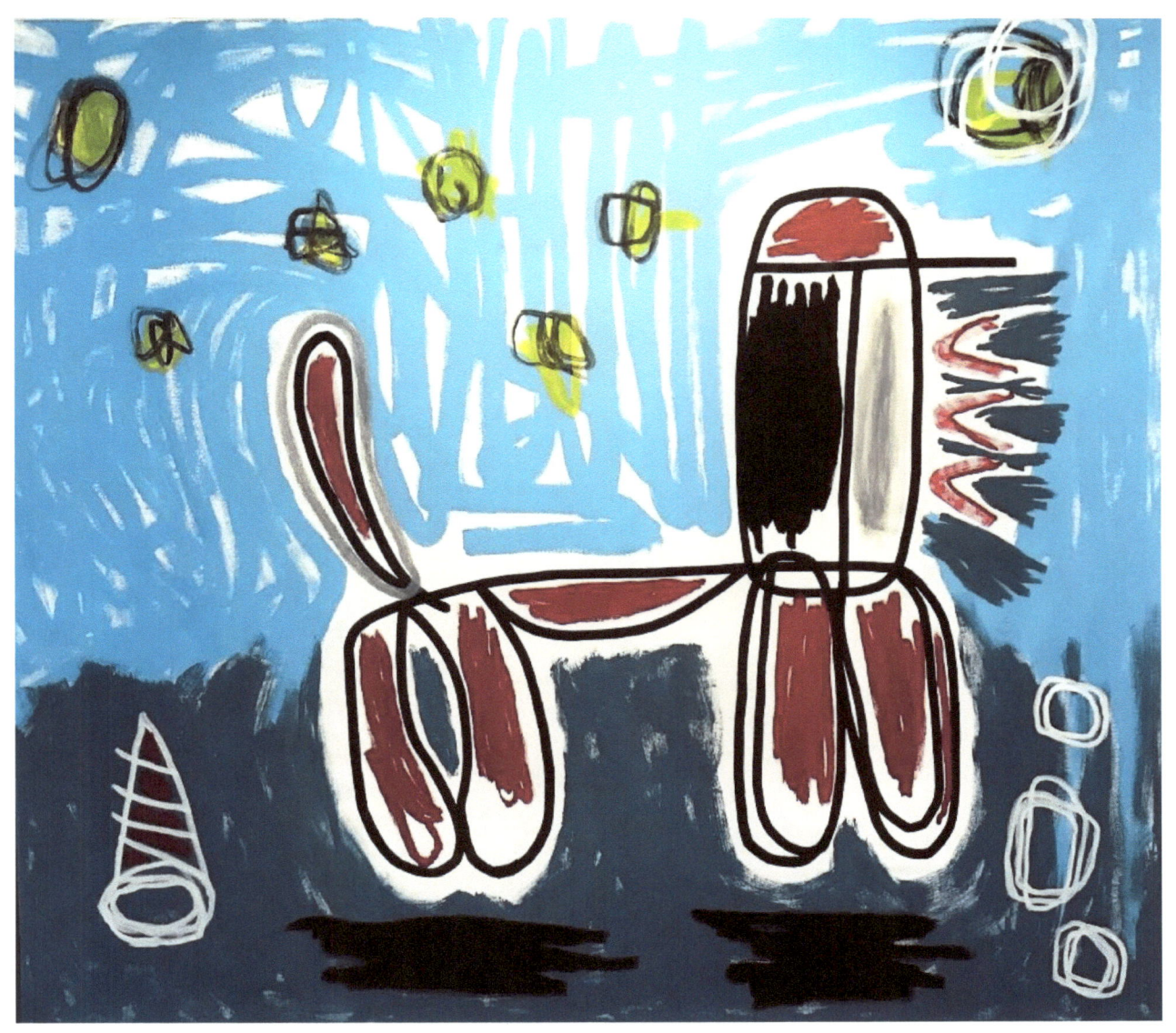

Red Balloon Puppy, 2019
Acrylic, latex, tempera on canvas
60 x 54 inches

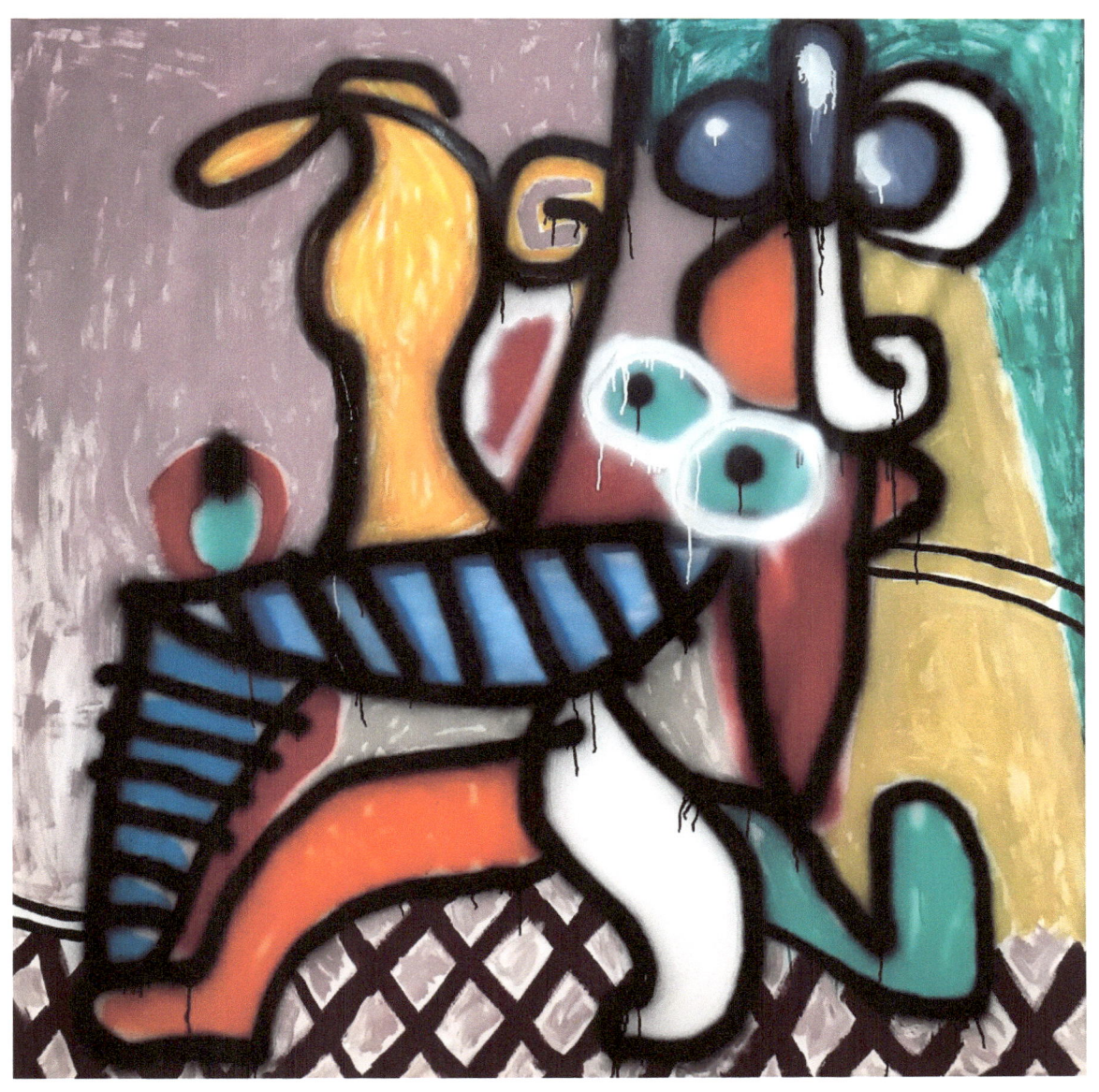

Large Still Life with Pedestal Table, 2020
Acrylic, spray paint, latex, tempera on canvas
60 x 60 inches

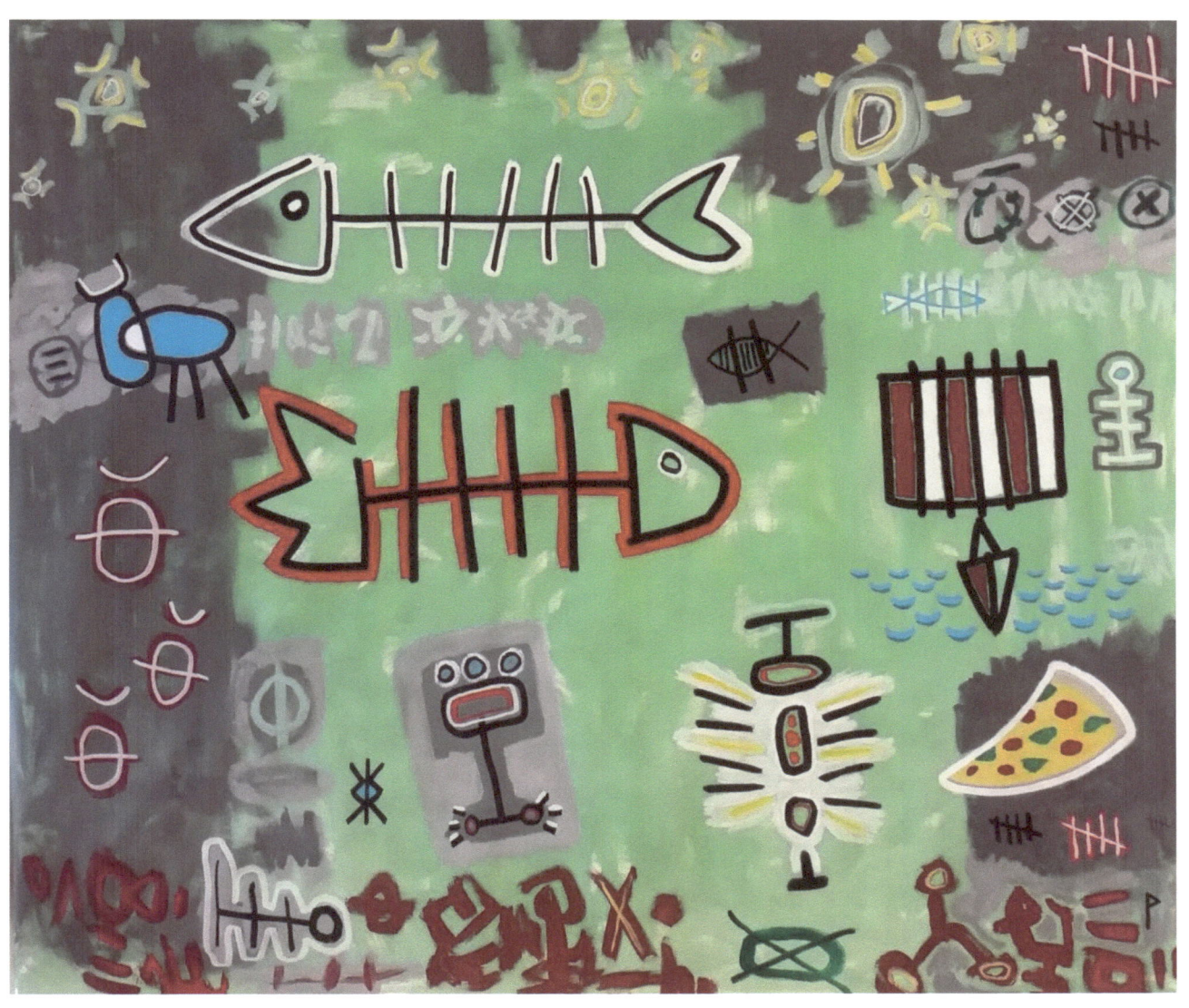

Did Vikings Dream Of Pizza?, 2016
Acrylic, latex, tempera on canvas
58 x 52 inches

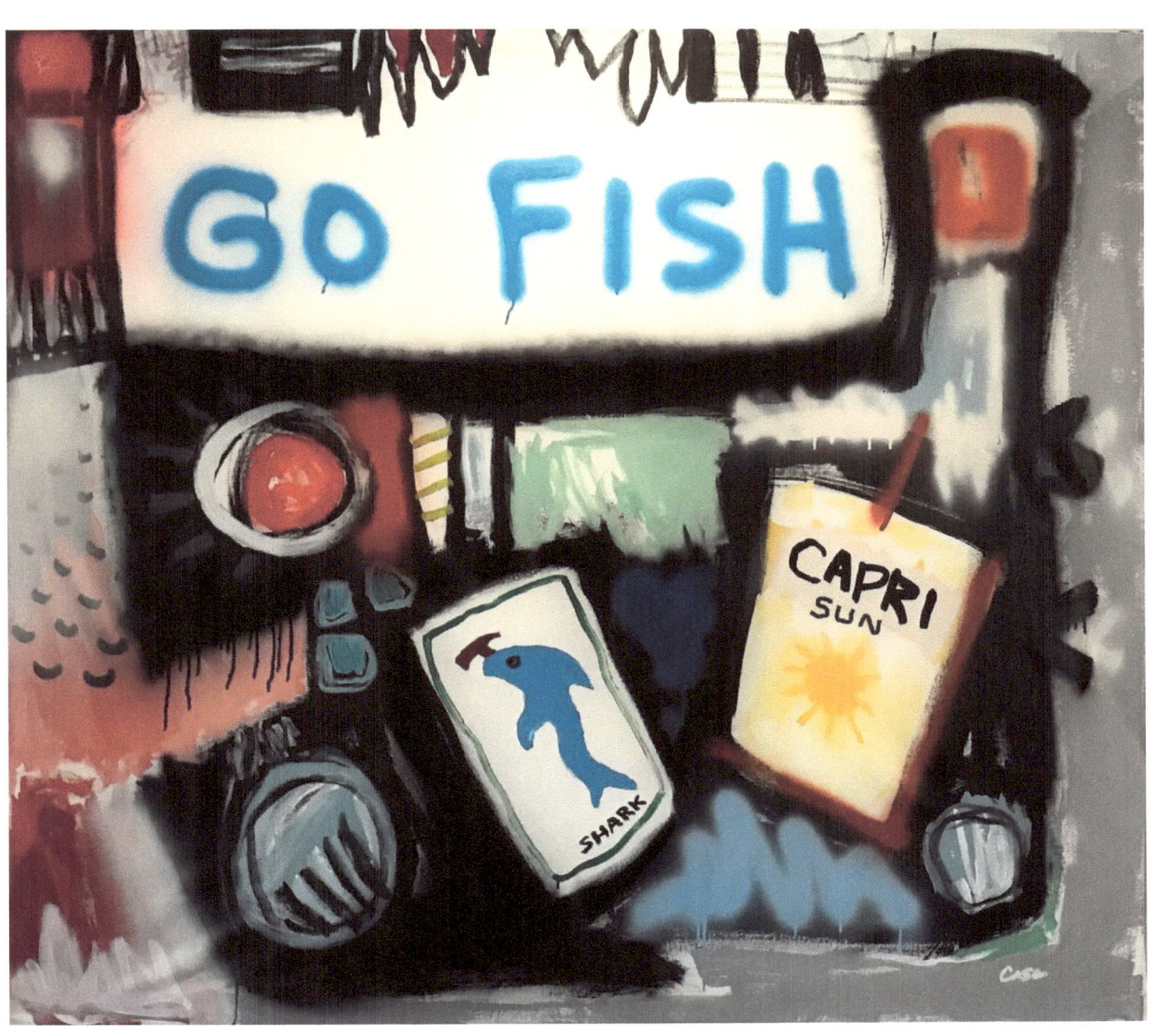

Go Fish, 2019
Acrylic, latex, spray paint, tempera on canvas
60 x 54 inches

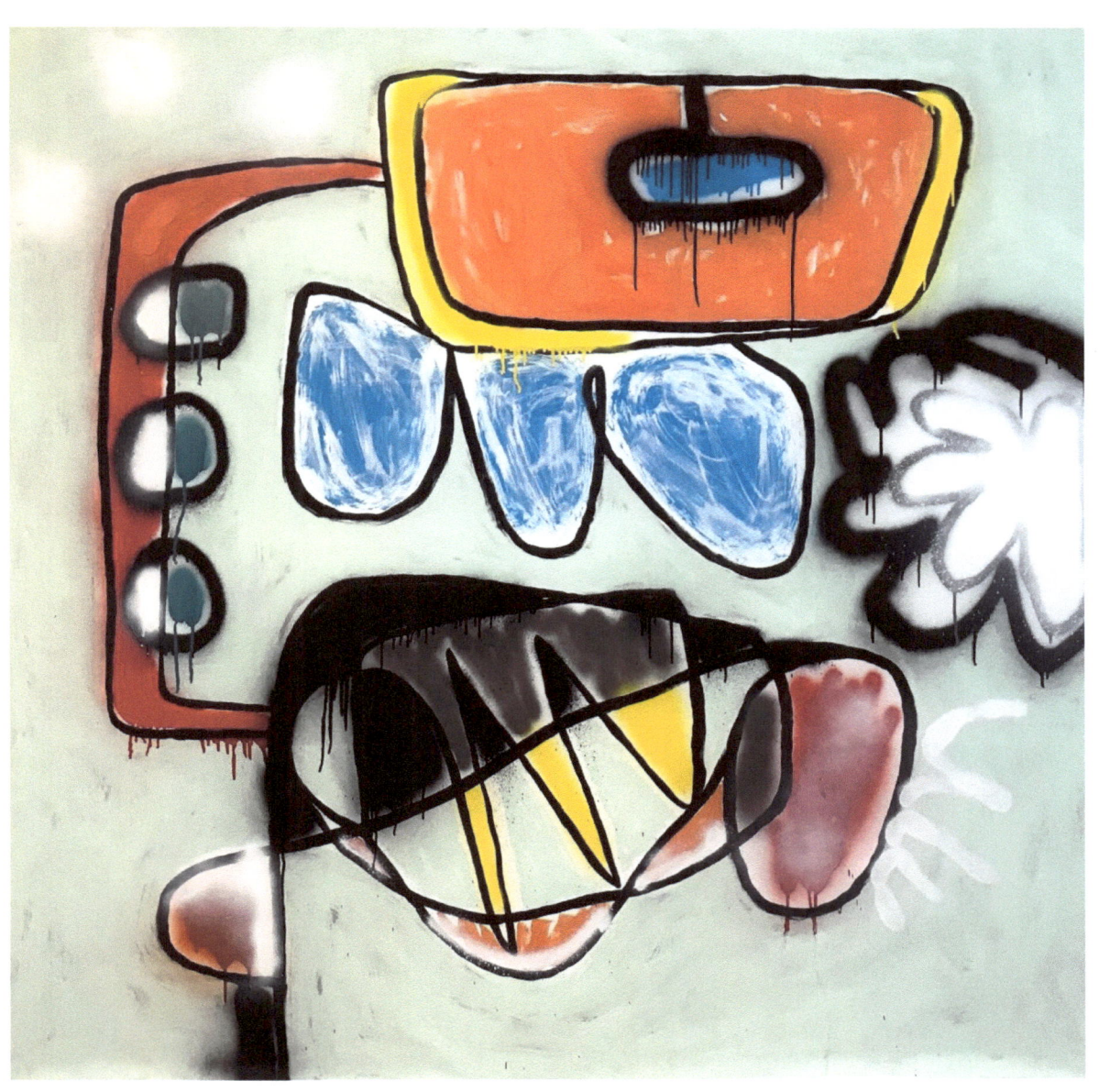

Untitled, 2020
Acrylic, latex, spray paint, tempera on canvas
60 x 60 inches

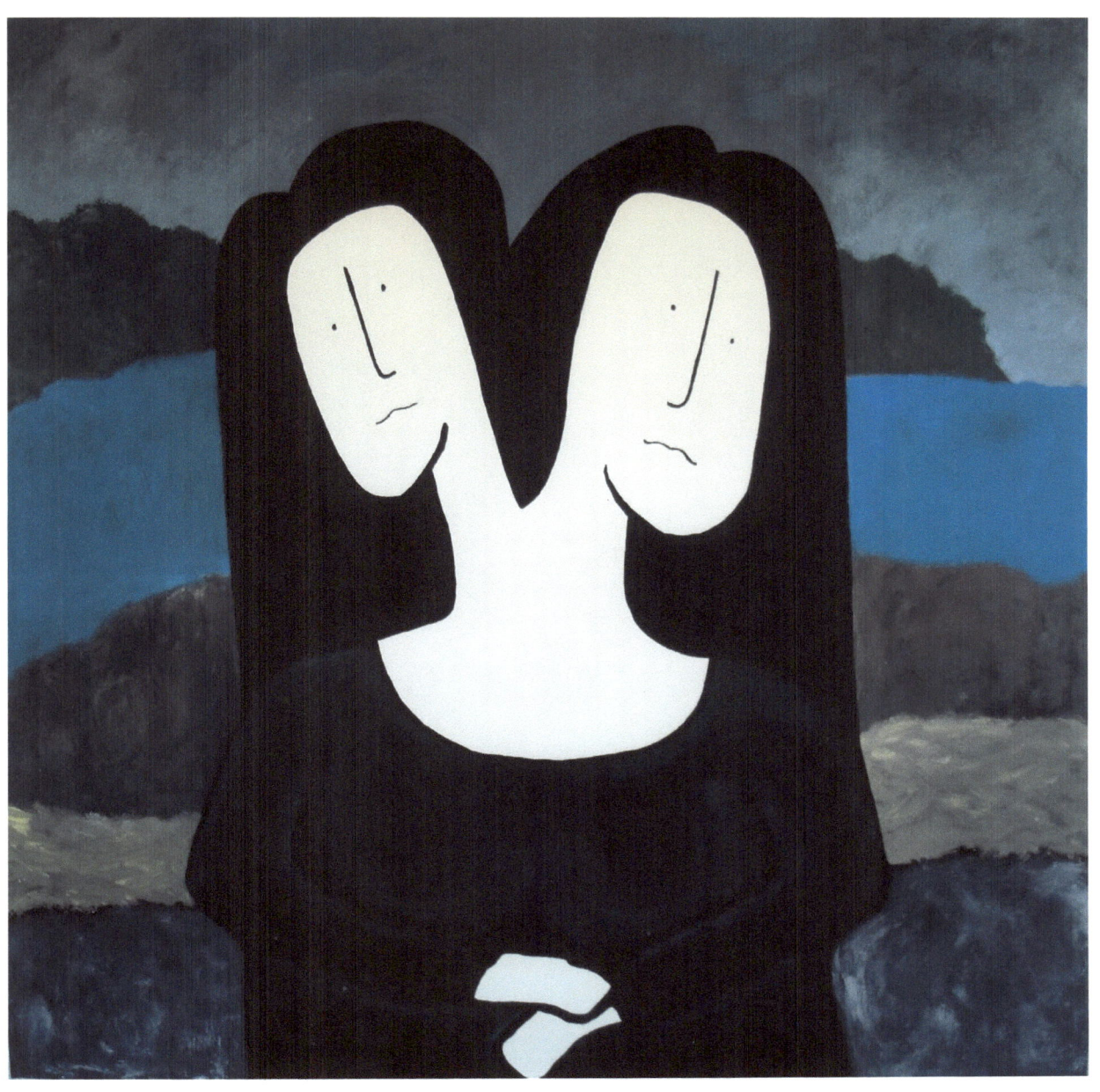

Two Headed Mona Lisa, 2010
Acrylic on wood panel
48 x 48 inches

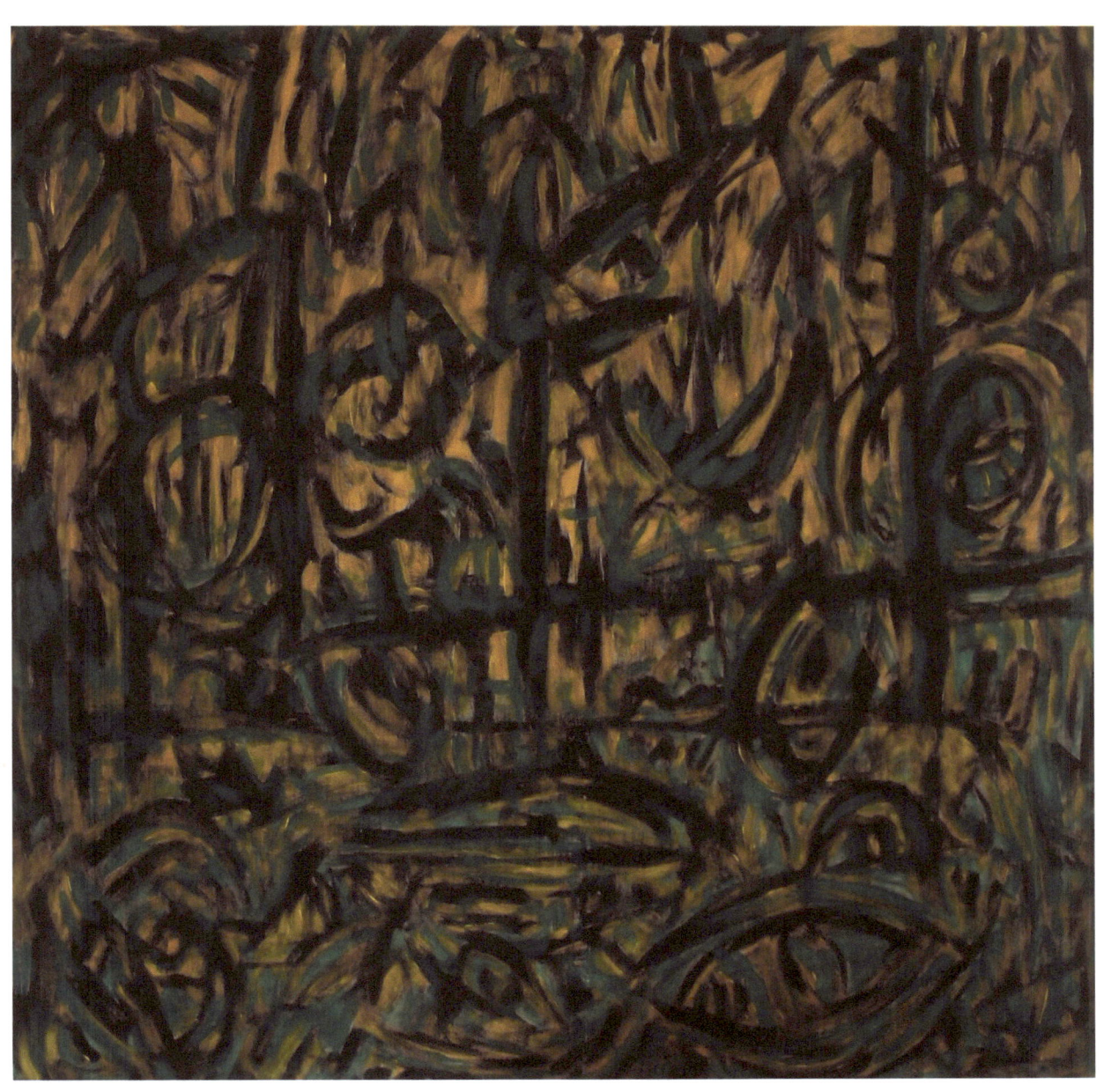

Panda Robot Kayak Bamboo Forest, 2010
Acrylic on wood panel
48 x 48 inches

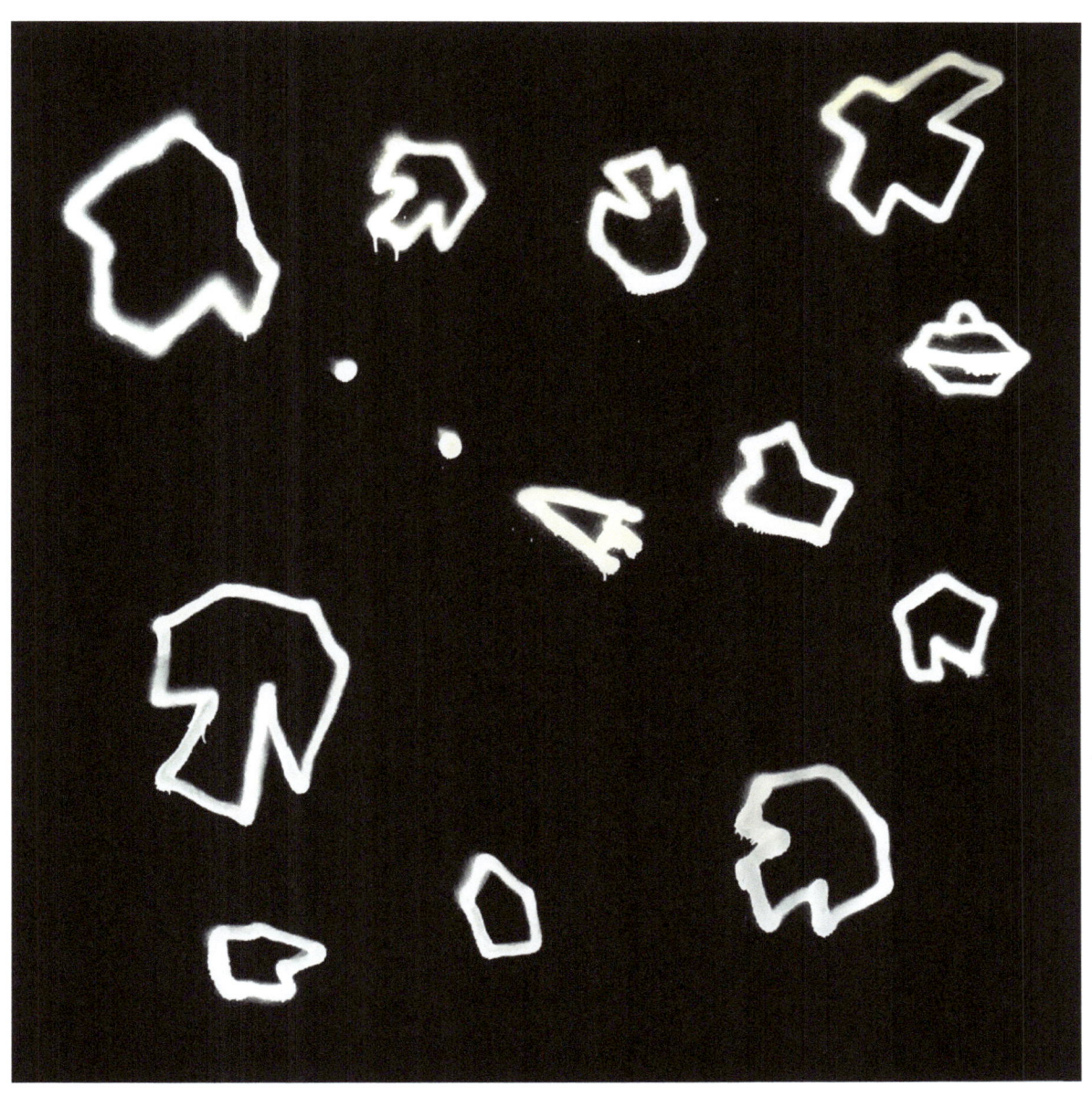

Asteroids, 2019
Acrylic, latex, spray paint on canvas
60 x 60 inches

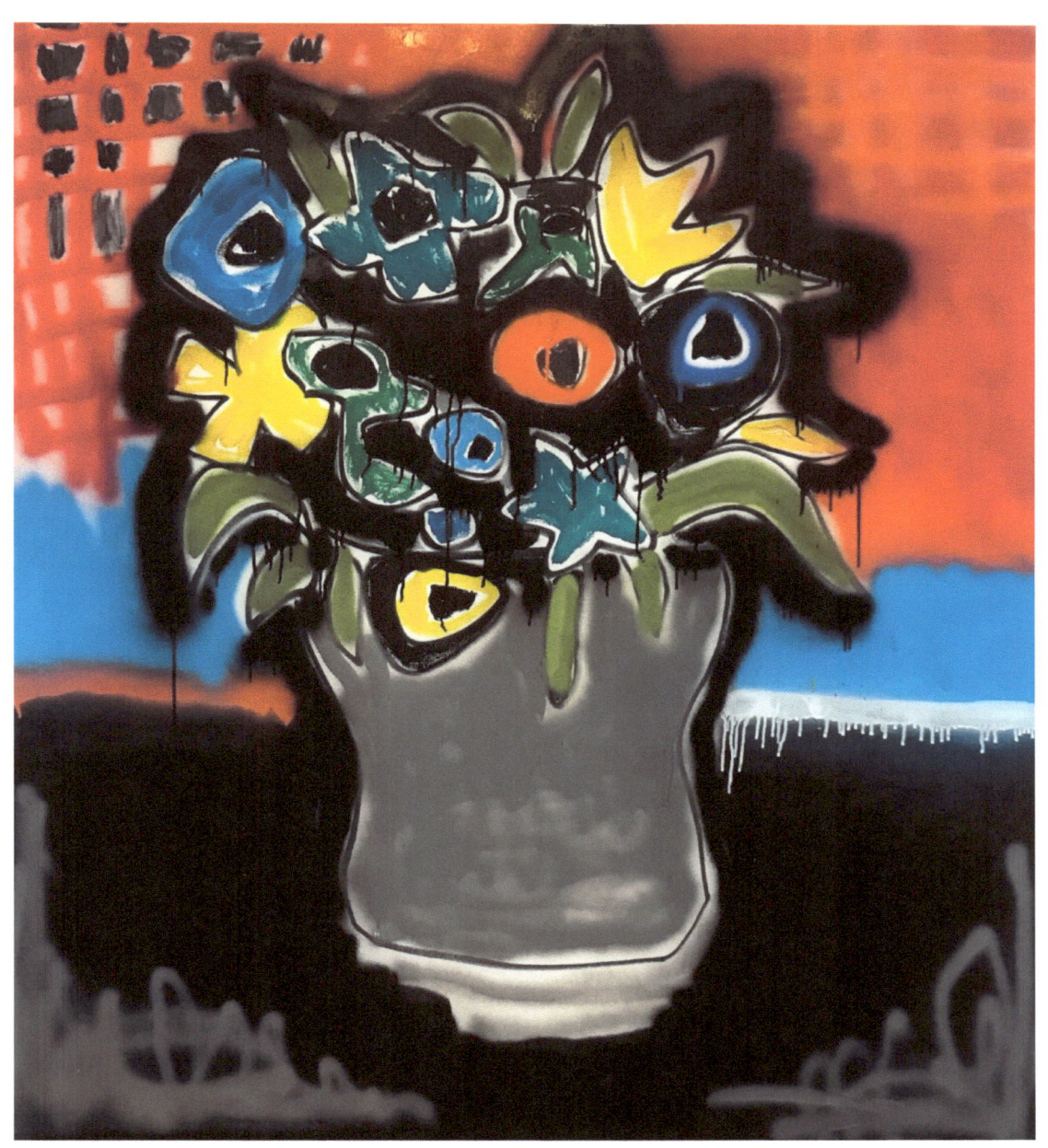

Still Life Flowers, 2019
Acrylic, latex, spray paint, tempera on canvas
54 x 60 inches

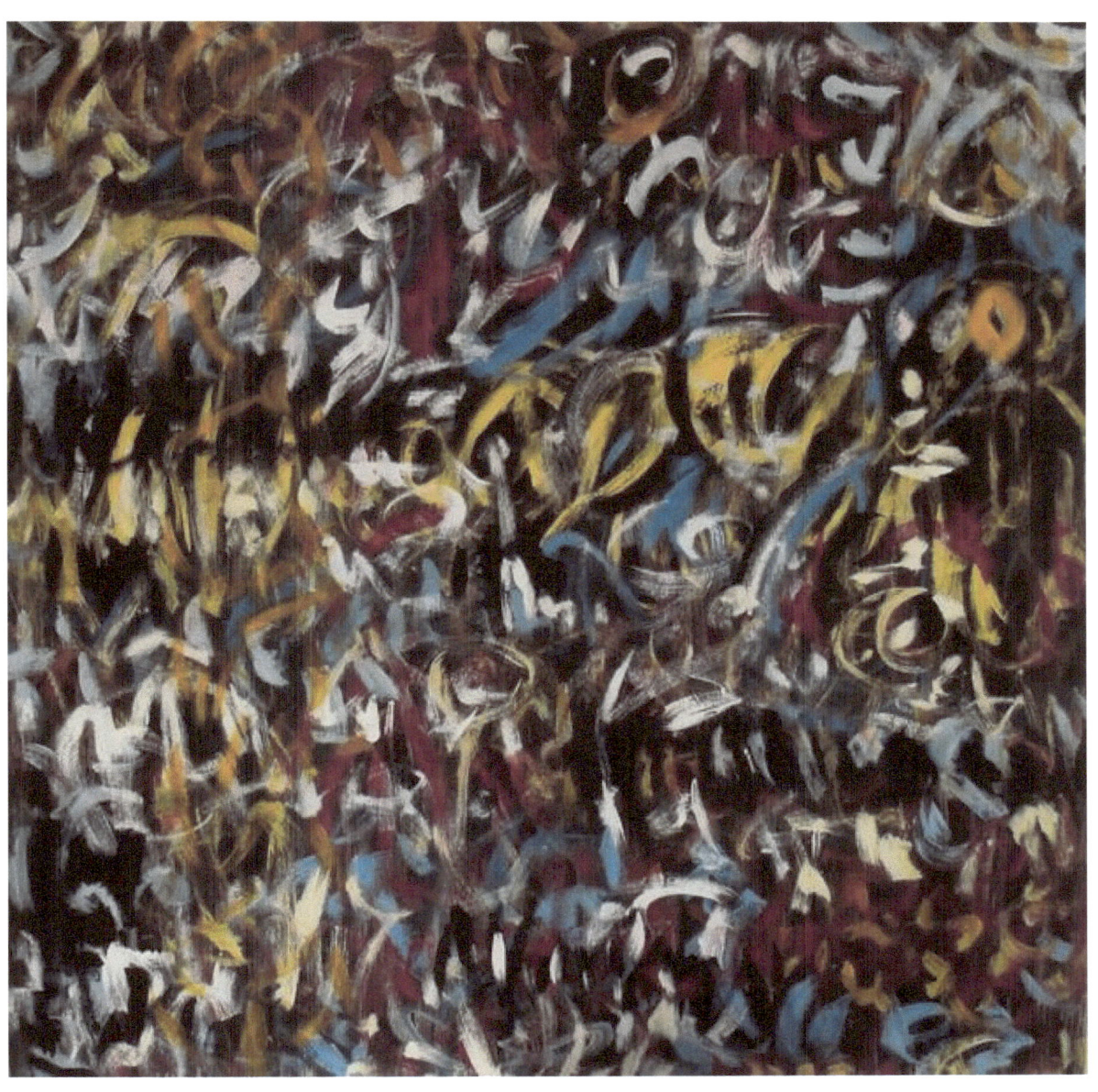

Urban Sanskrit, 2010
Acrylic on wood panel
48 x 48 inches

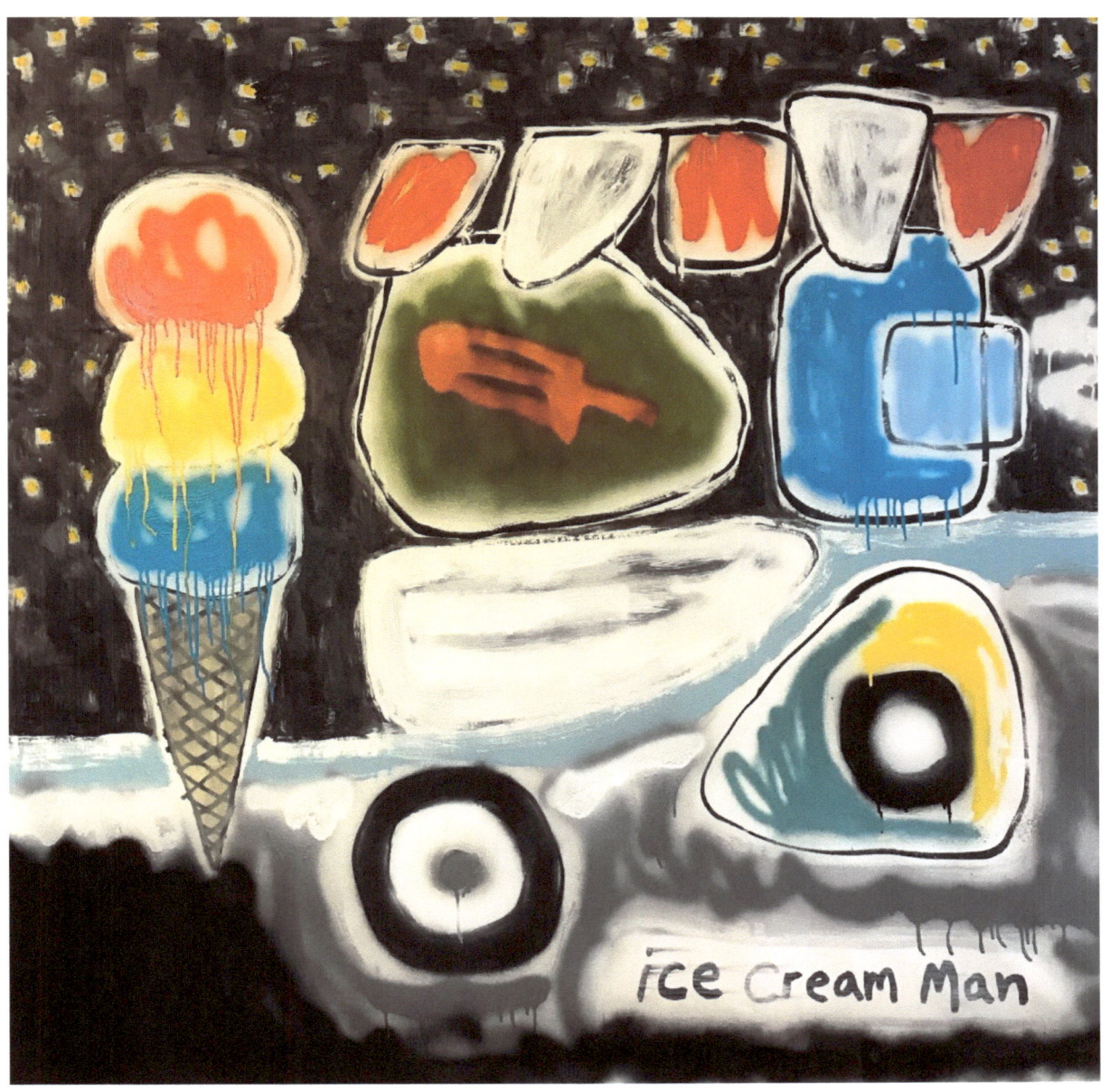

Ice Cream Man, 2019
Acrylic, latex, spray paint on canvas
60 x 60 inches

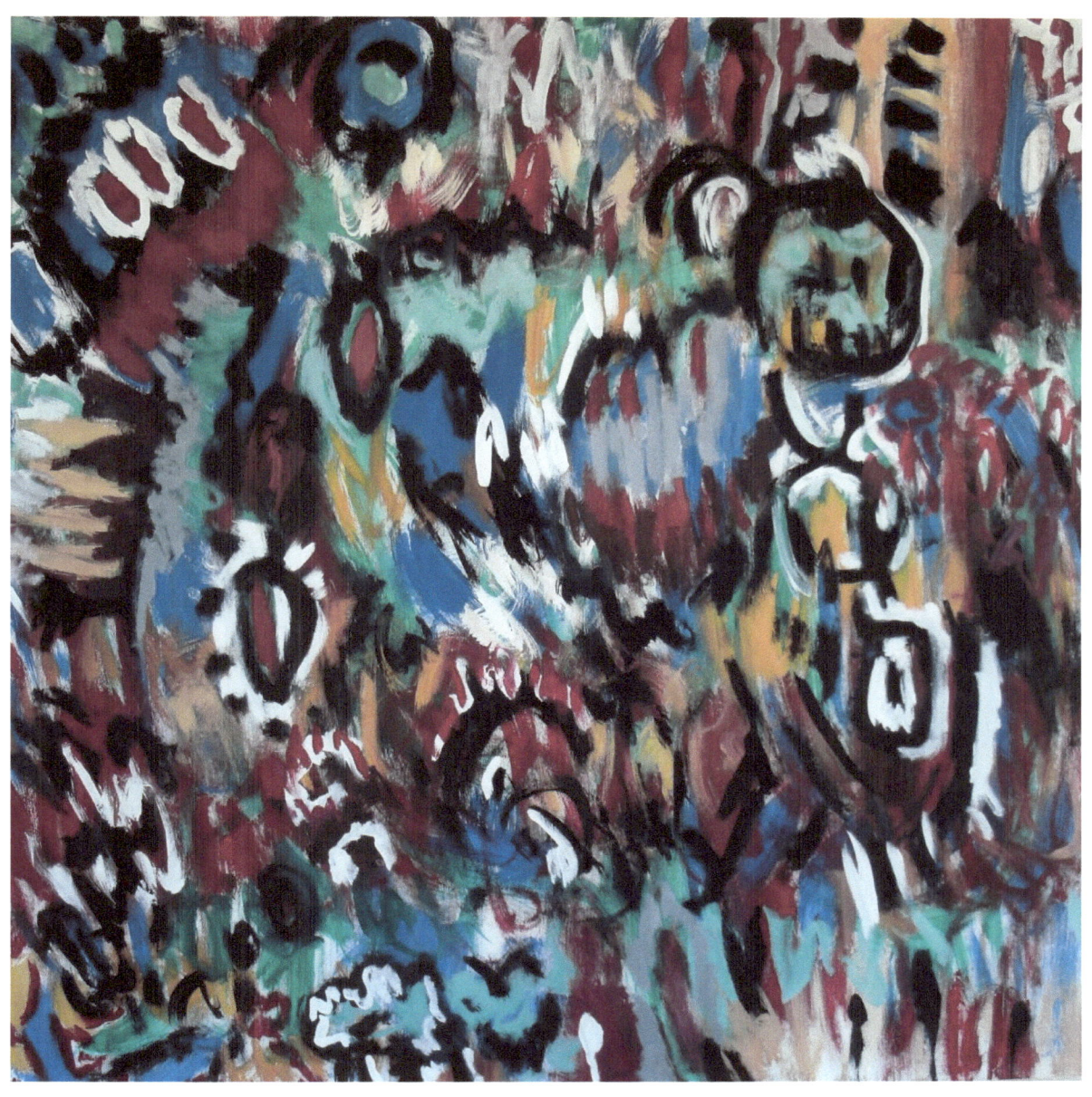

Jezebel and Zeus, 2010
Acrylic on wood panel
48 x 48 inches

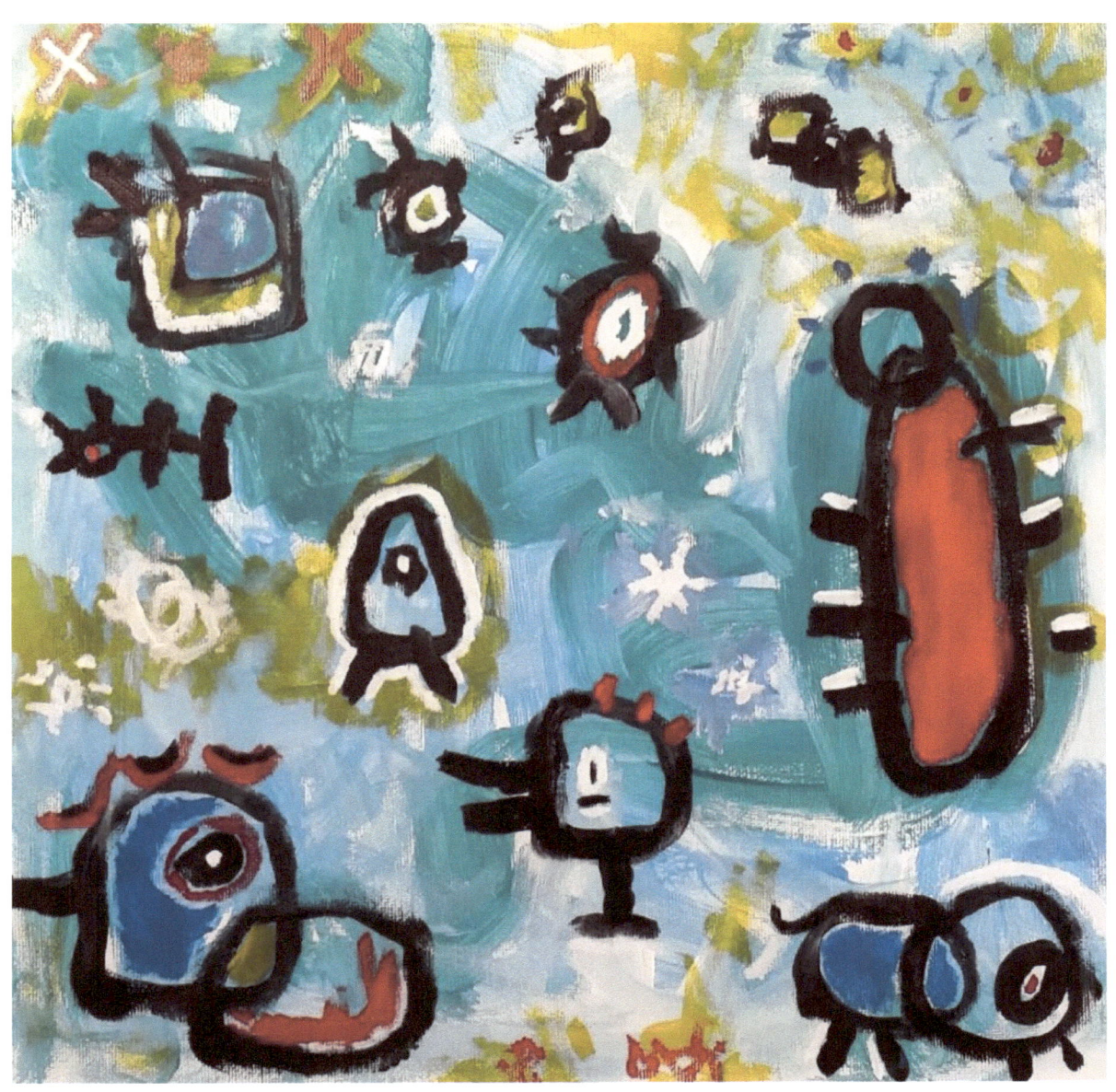

Red Green 1.9, 2016
Acrylic on canvas board
12 x 12 inches

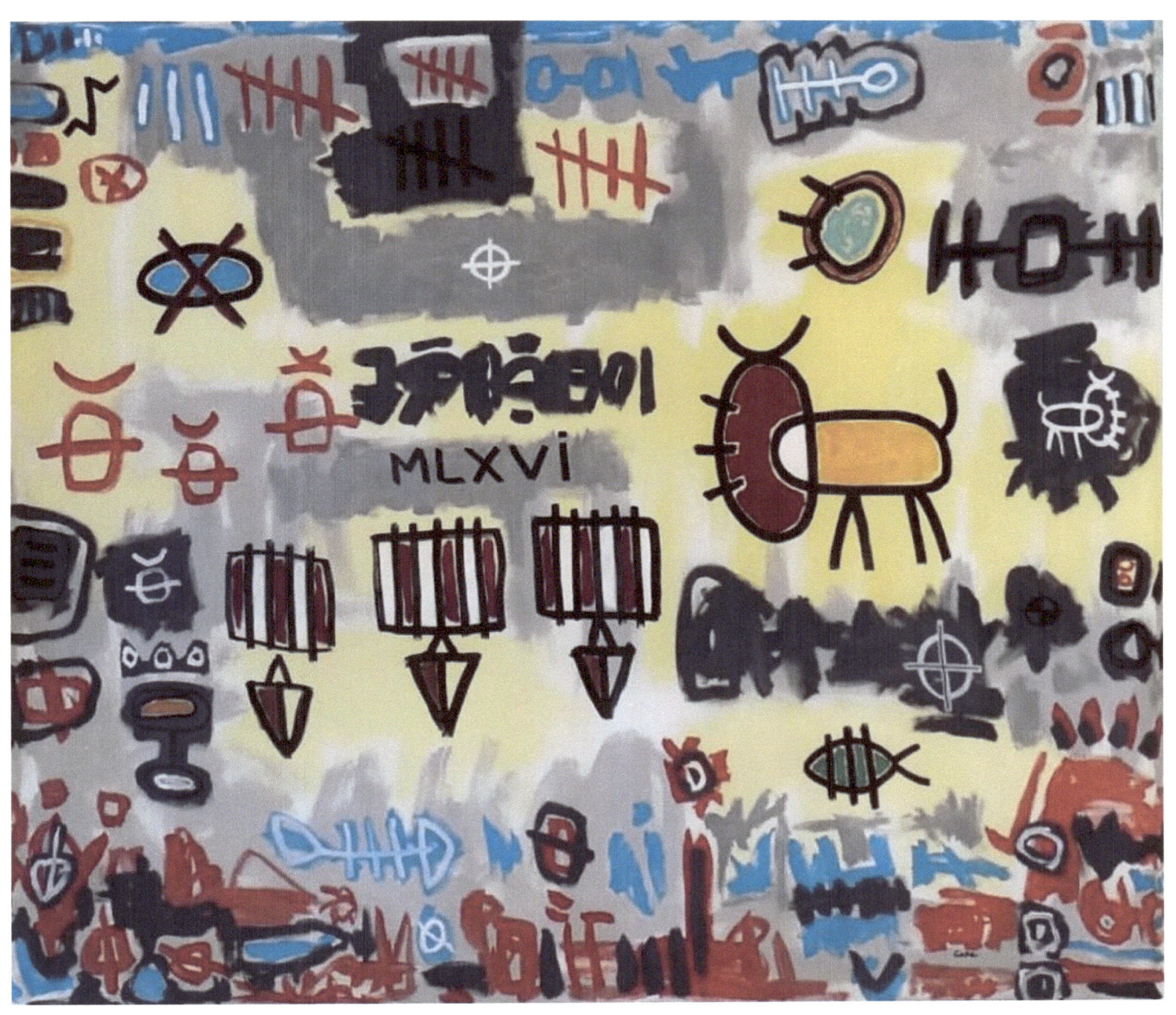

***Viking Raid**, 2016
Acrylic, latex, tempera on canvas
60 x 54 inches

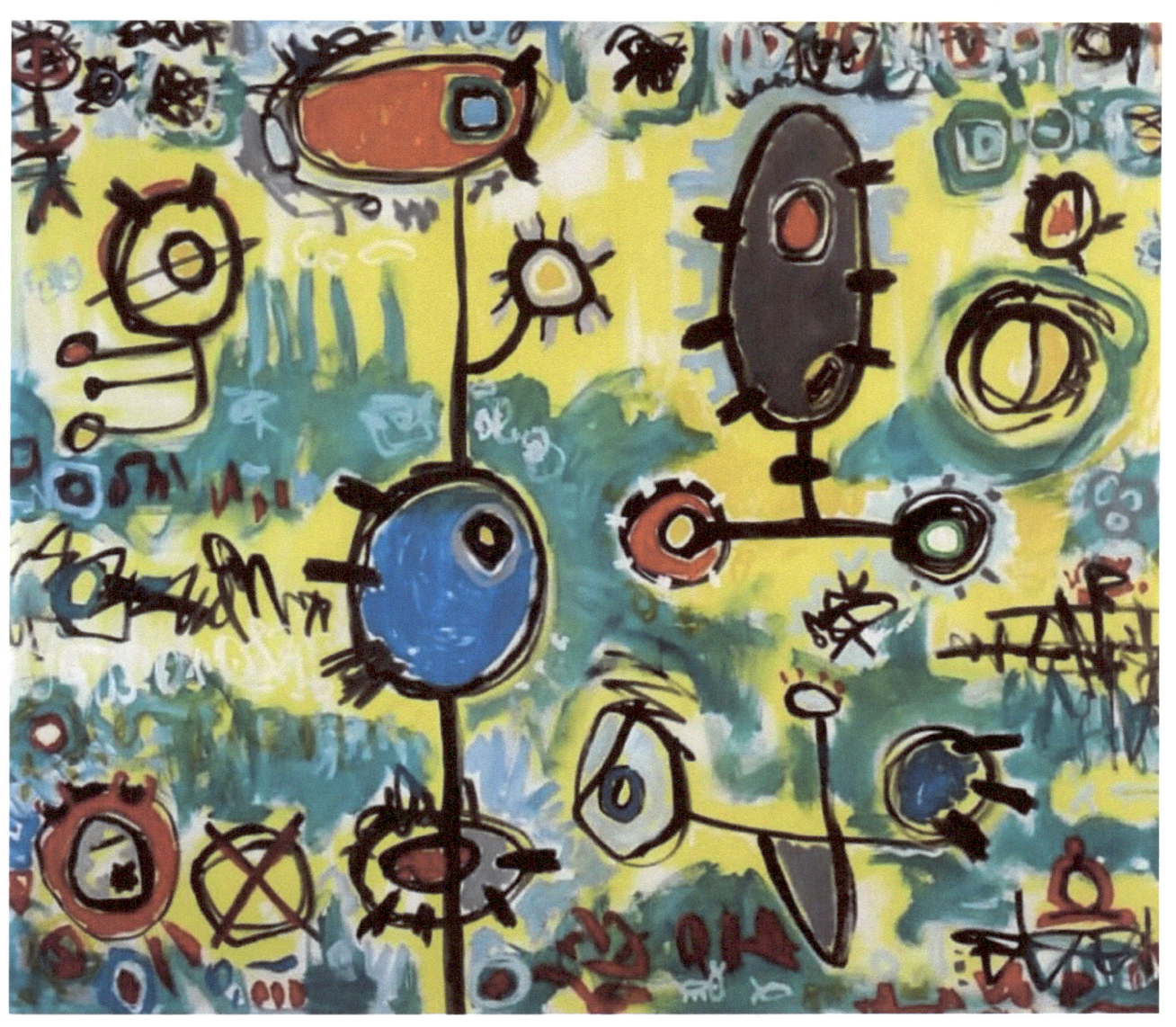

Future Robot Bird, 2016
Acrylic, latex, tempera on canvas
60 x 52 inches

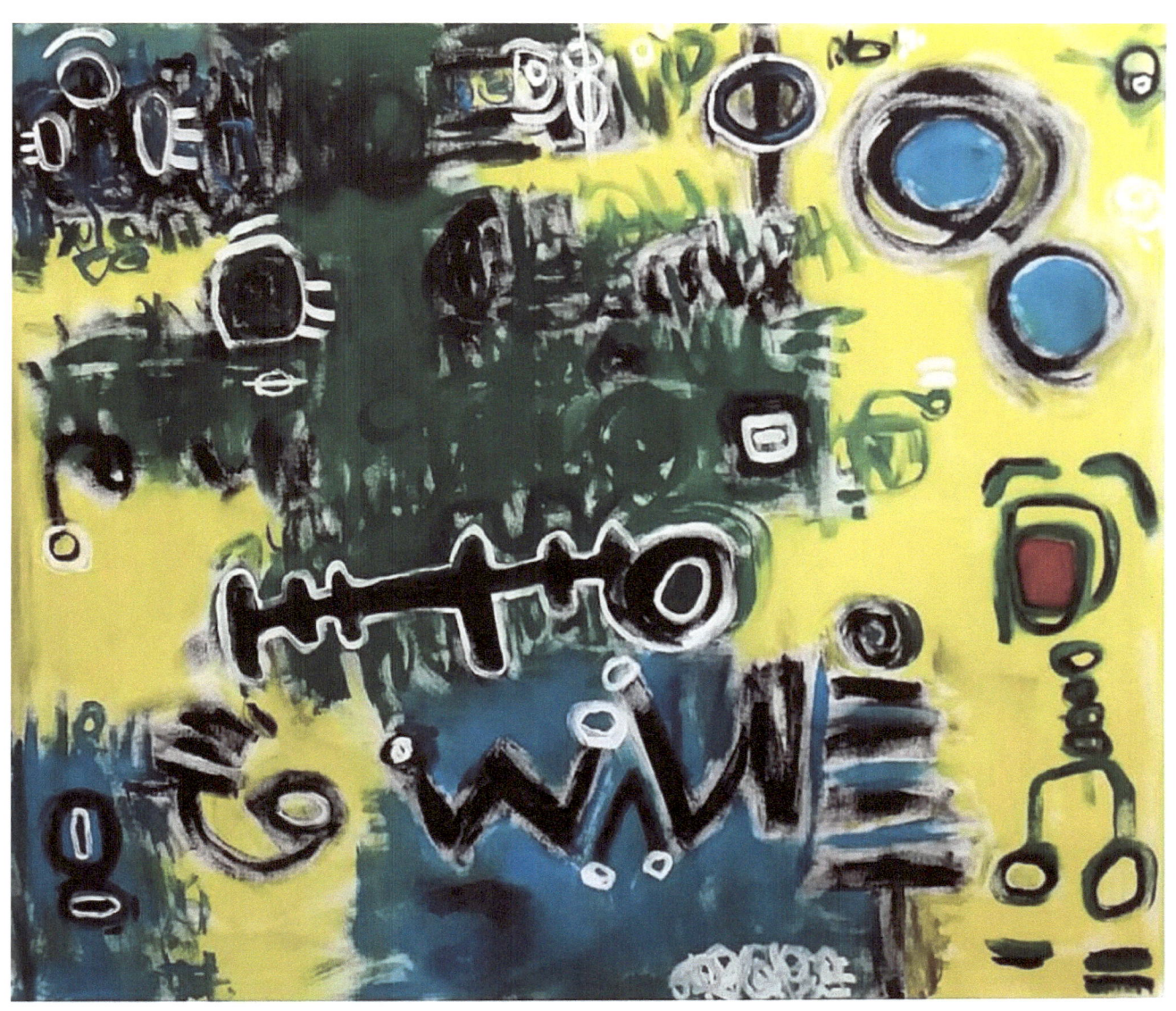

Green Yellow Red 6.4, 2015
Acrylic, latex, tempera on canvas
60 x 54 inches

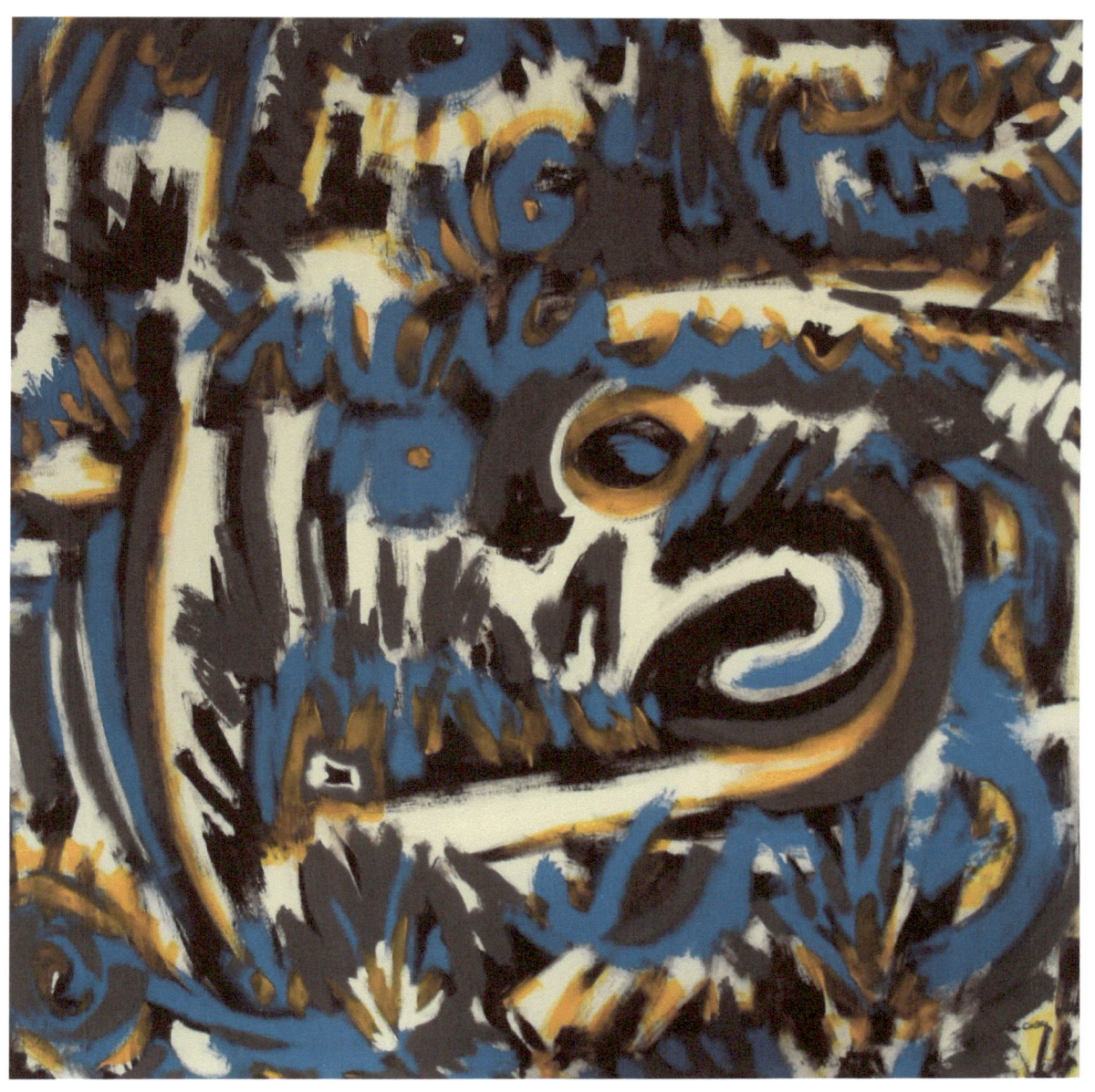

Self Portrait in Blue, 2010
Acrylic on wood panel
48 x 48 inches

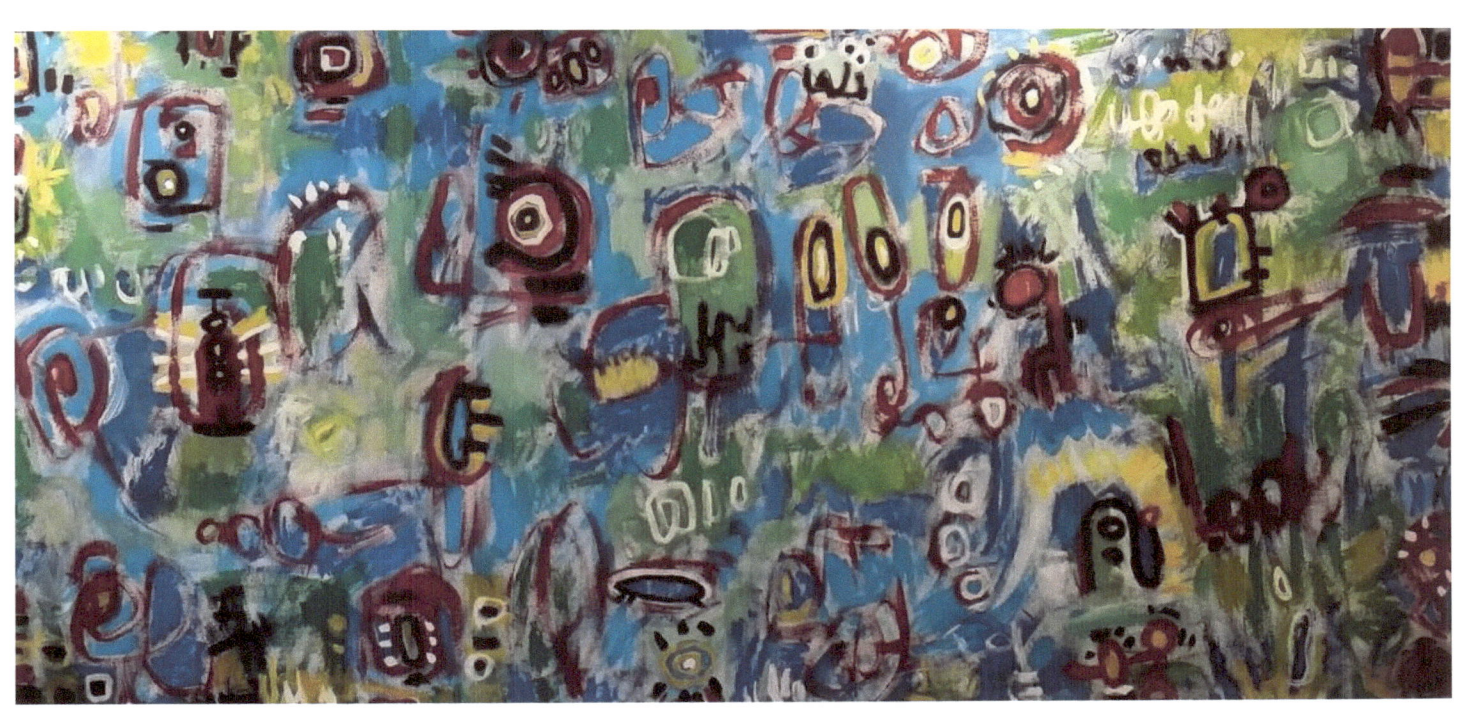

Blue Green 3.7, 2013
Acrylic, latex, tempera on canvas
96 x 48 inches

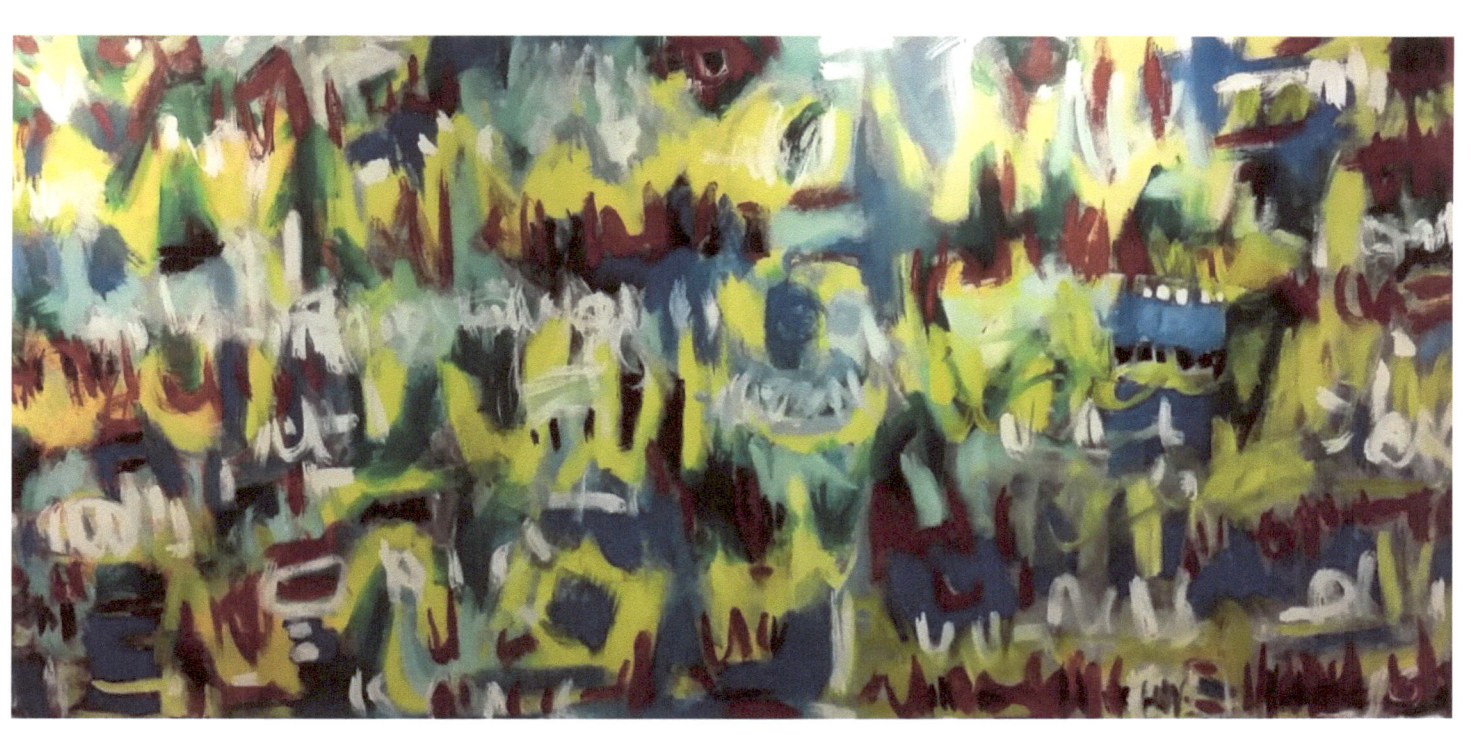

Yellow 1.9, 2013
Acrylic, latex, tempera on canvas
96 x 48 inches

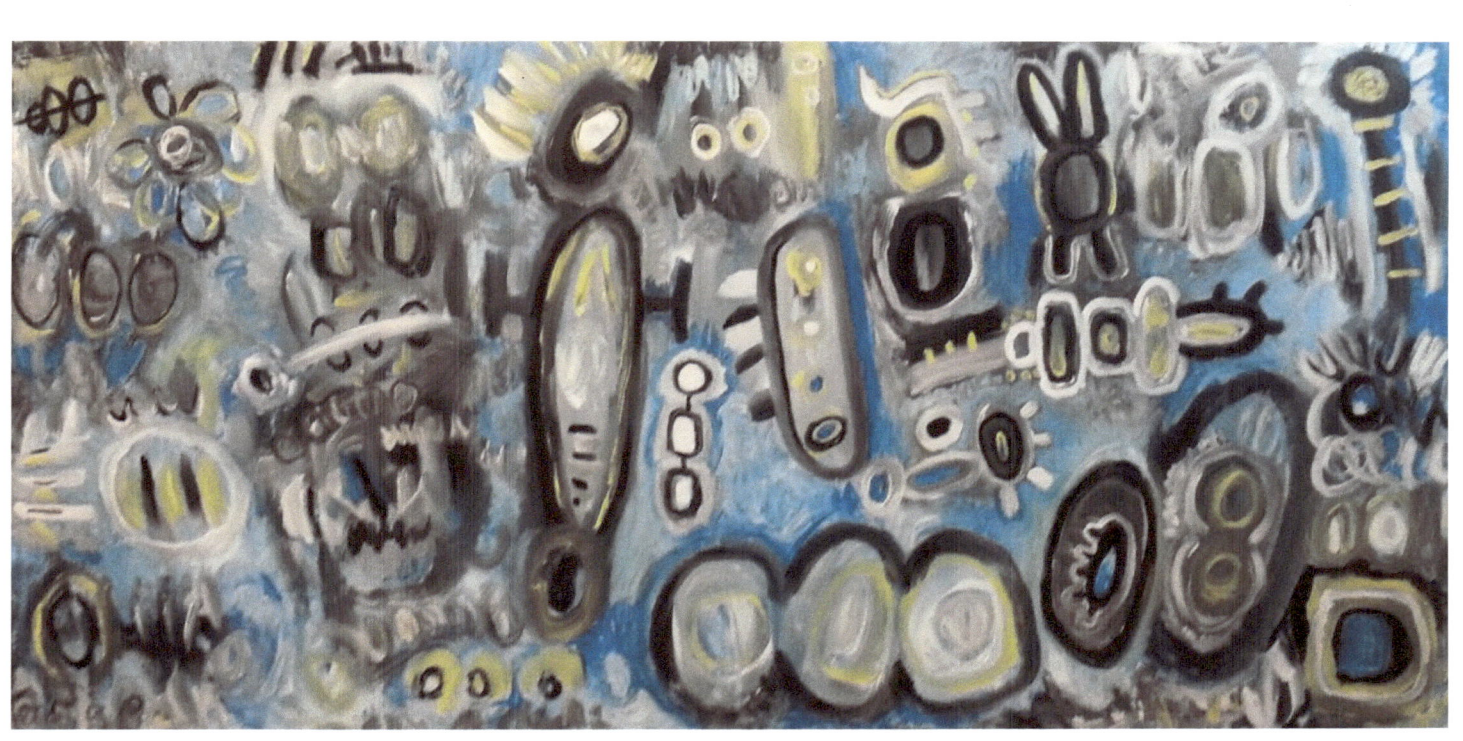

4.6, 2013
Acrylic, latex, tempera on canvas
96 x 48 inches

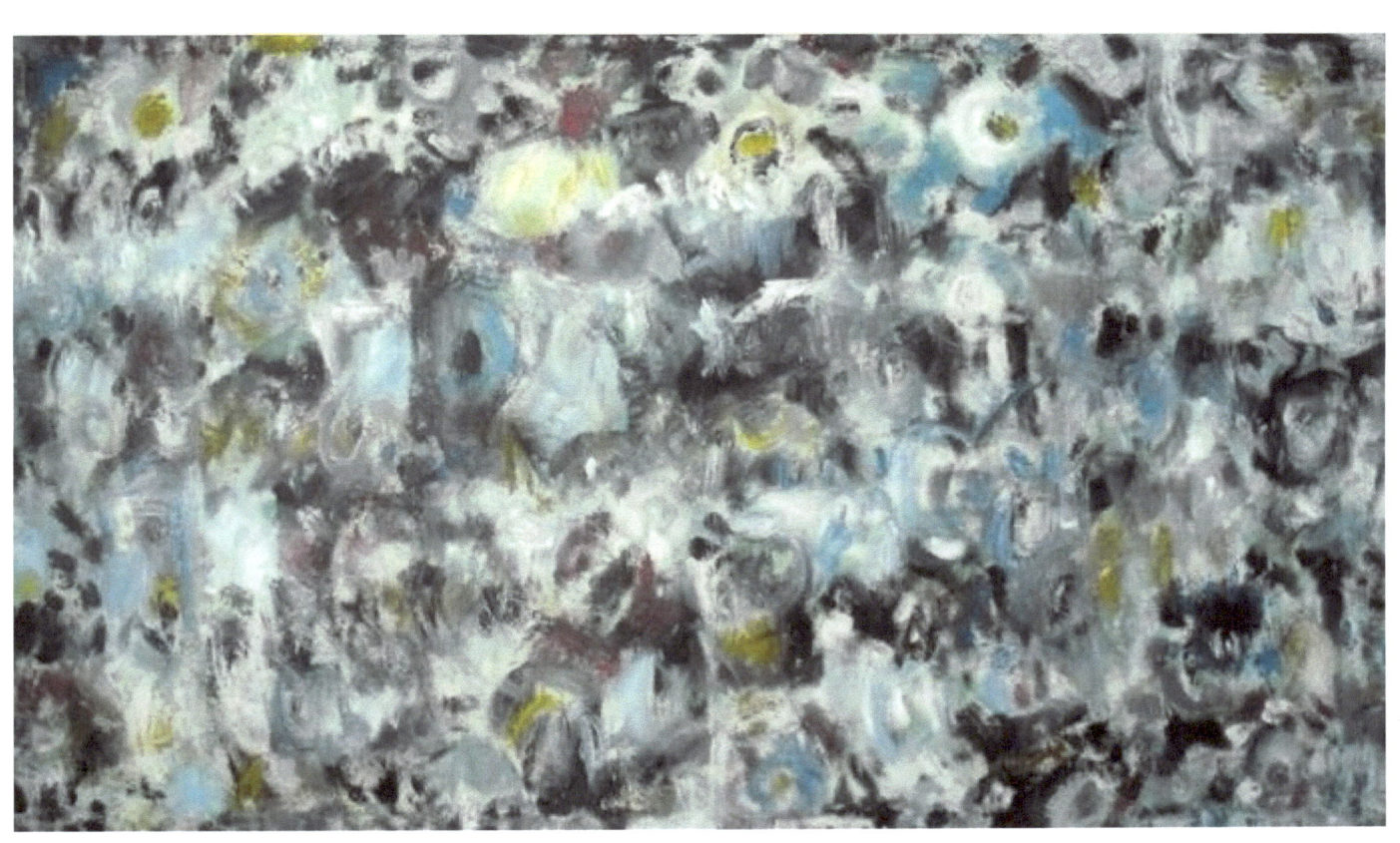

1.9, 2013
Acrylic, latex, tempera on canvas
60 x 36 inches

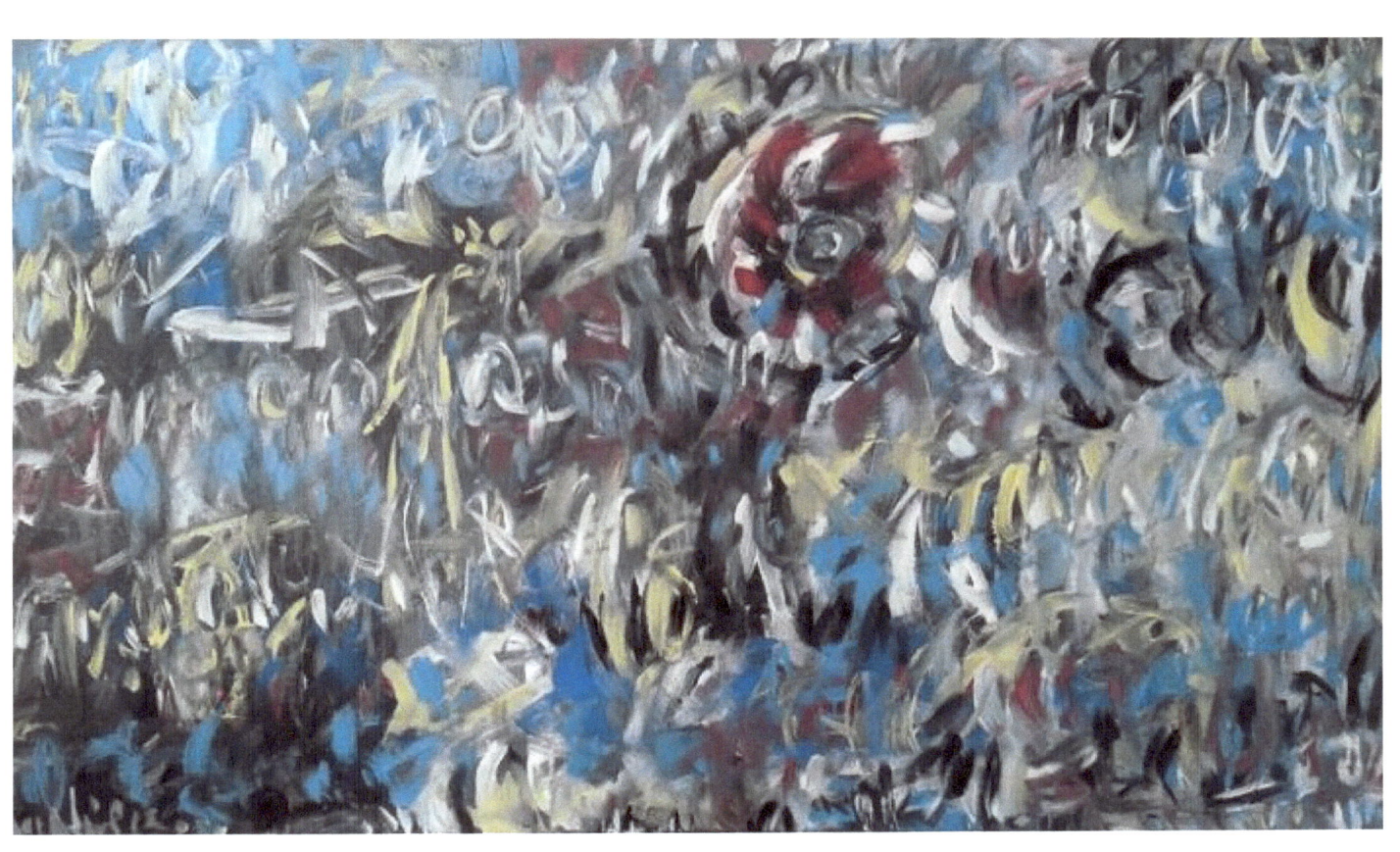

7.3, 2013
Acrylic, latex, tempera on canvas
60 x 36 inches

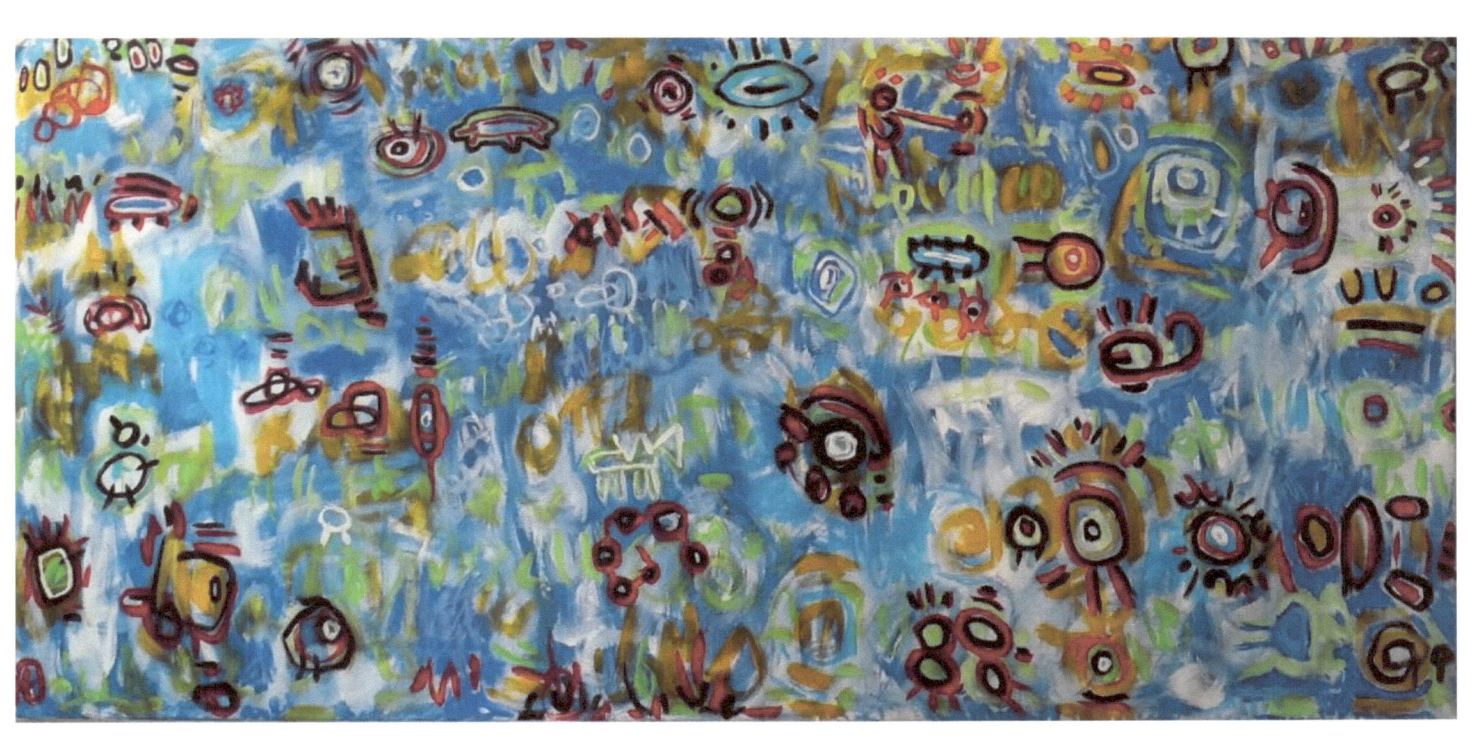

Blue Yellow 2.8, 2013
Acrylic, latex, tempera on canvas
96 x 48 inches

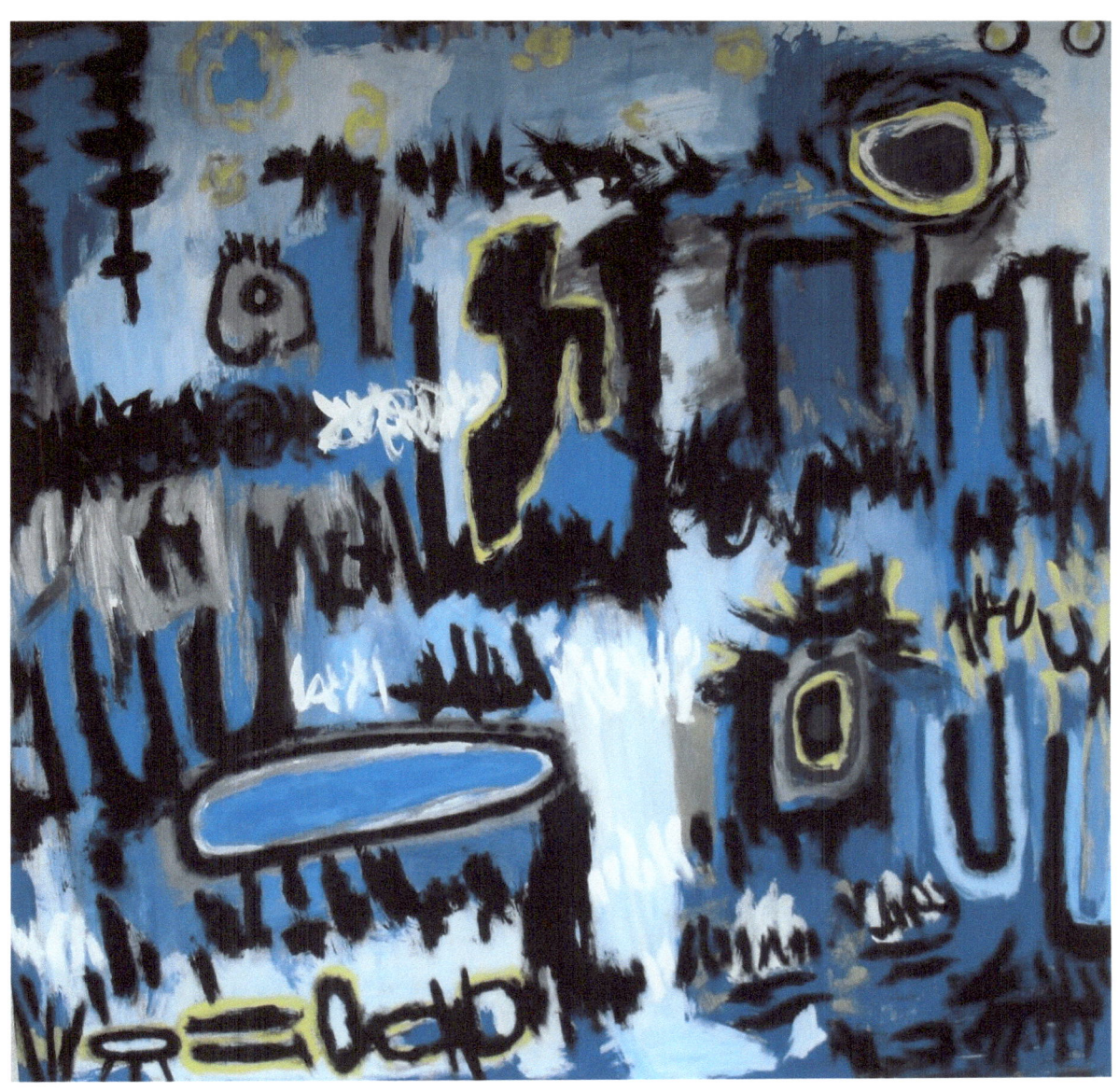

Midnight Clouds, 2011
Acrylic on wood panel
48 x 48 inches

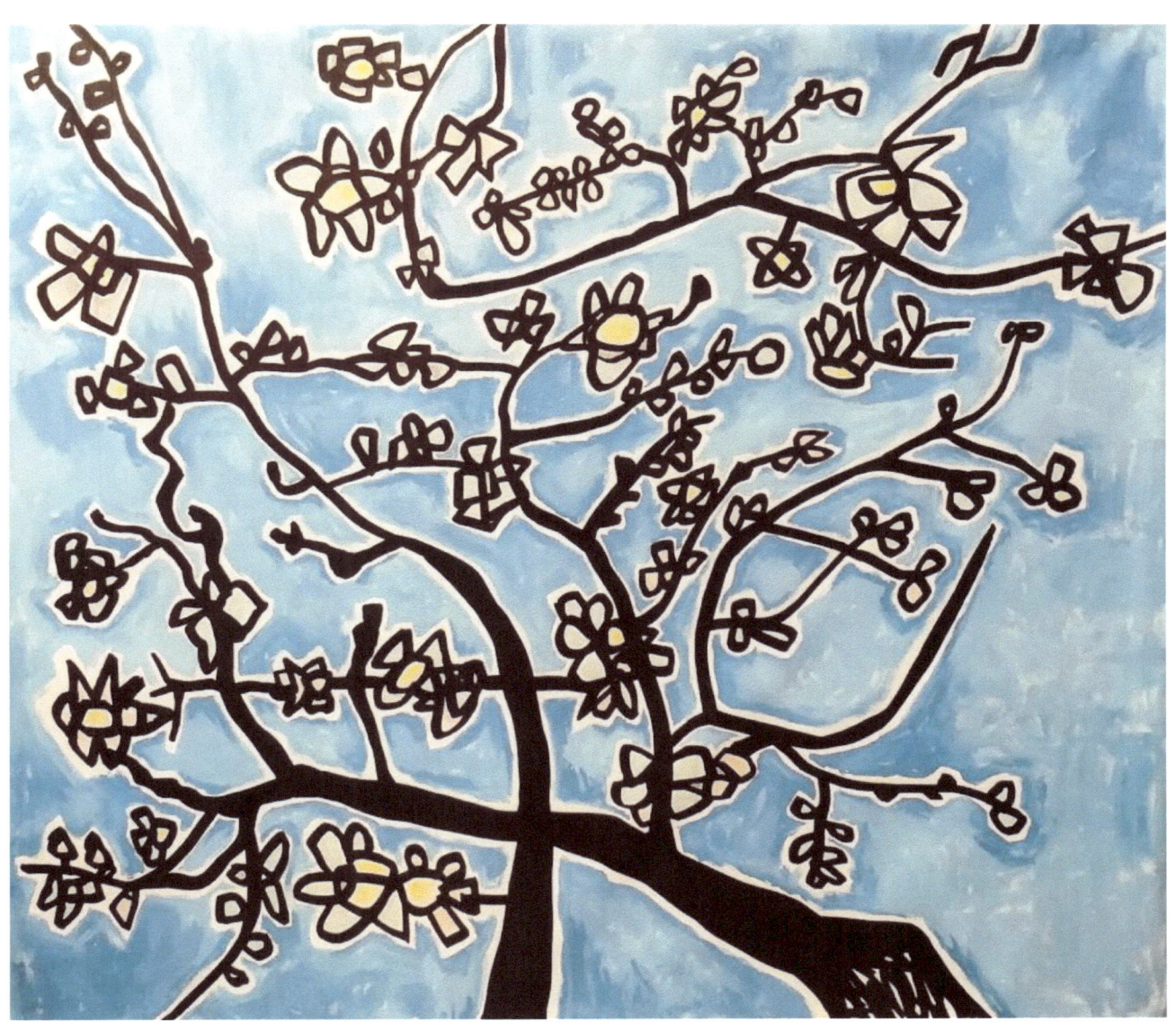

Almond Blossom, 2016
Acrylic, latex, tempera on canvas
60 x 54 inches

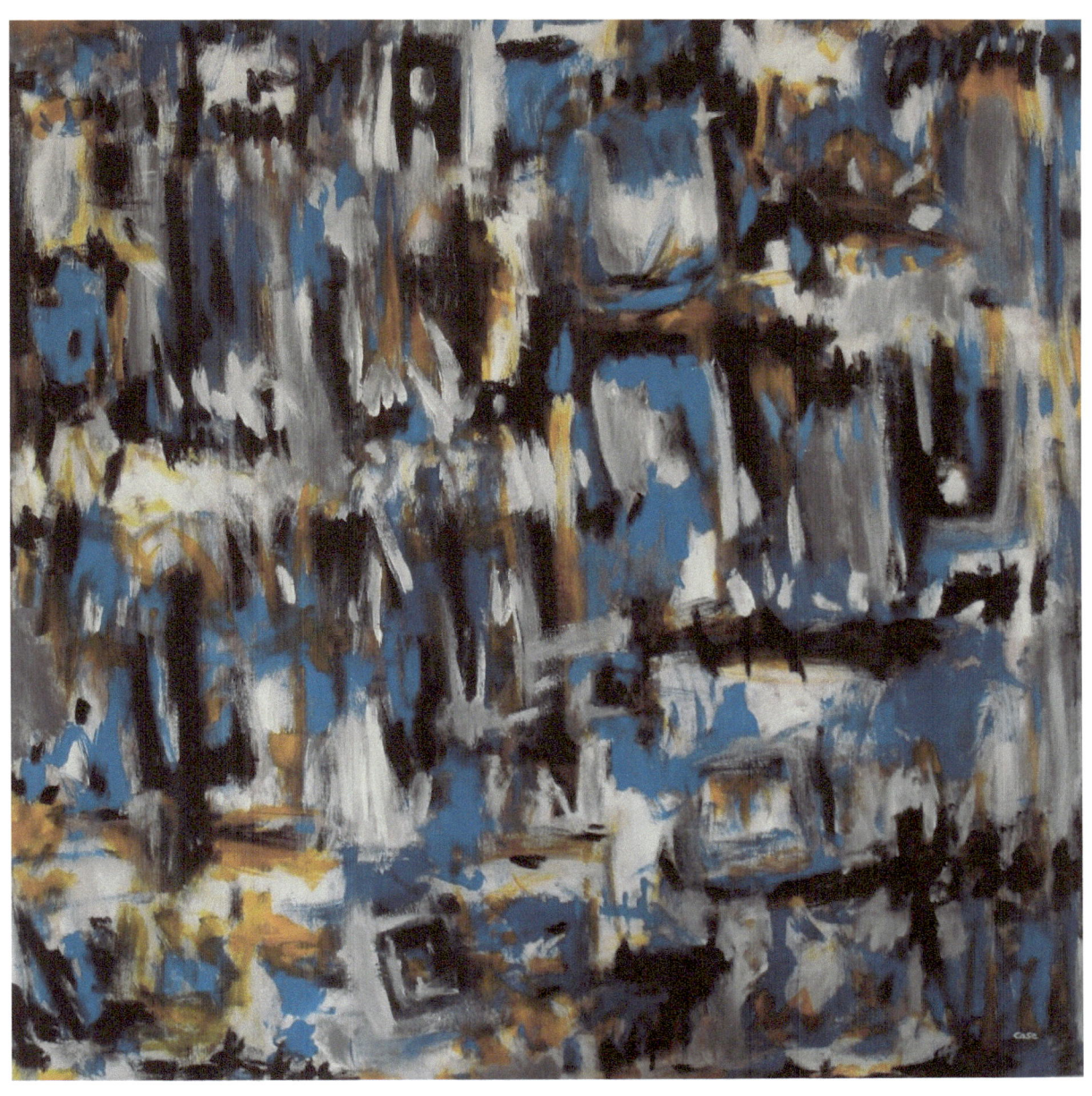

Blue Desert Bird, 2010
Acrylic on wood panel
48 x 48 inches

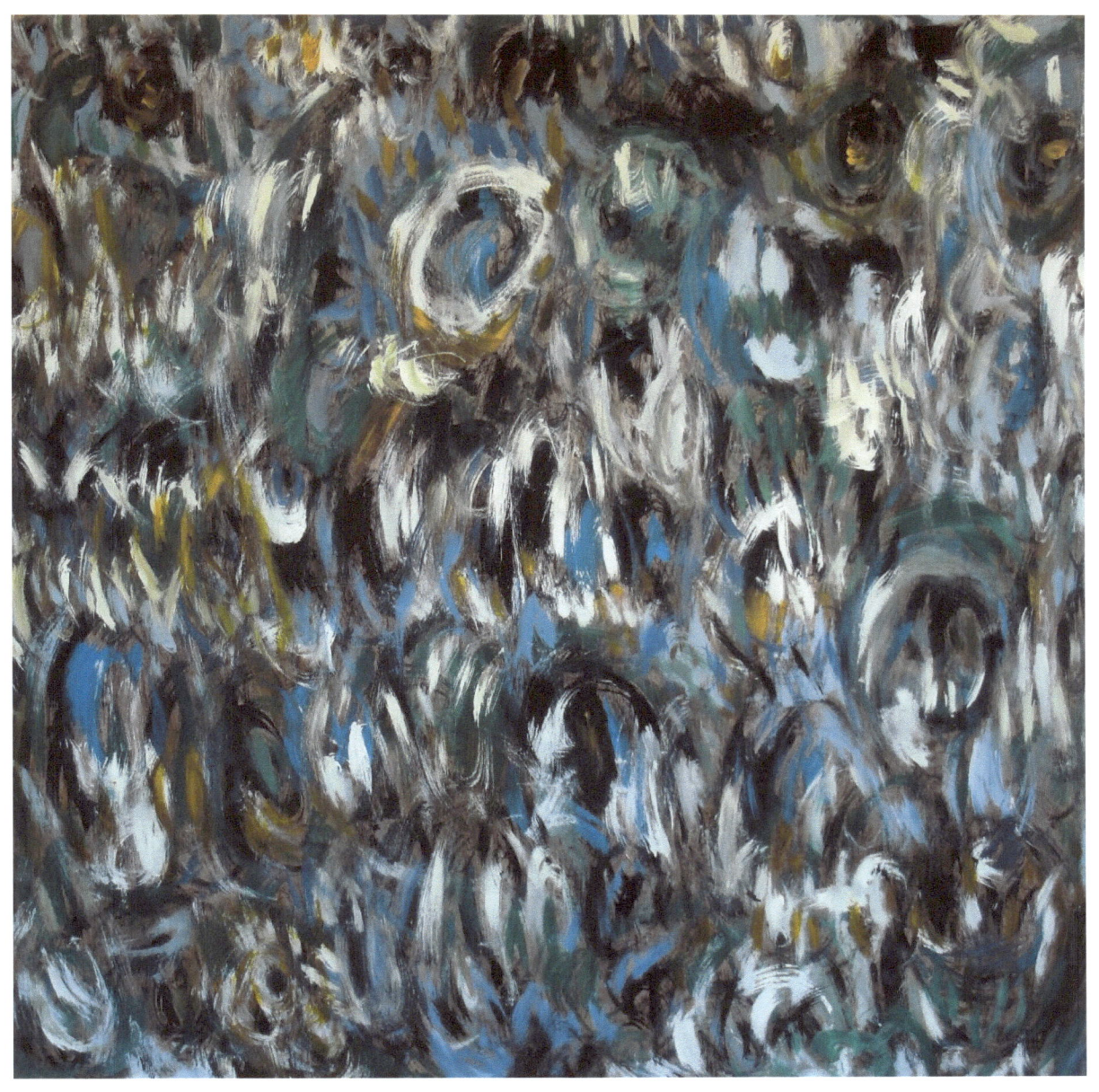

Wind Garden, 2010
Acrylic on wood panel
48 x 48 inches

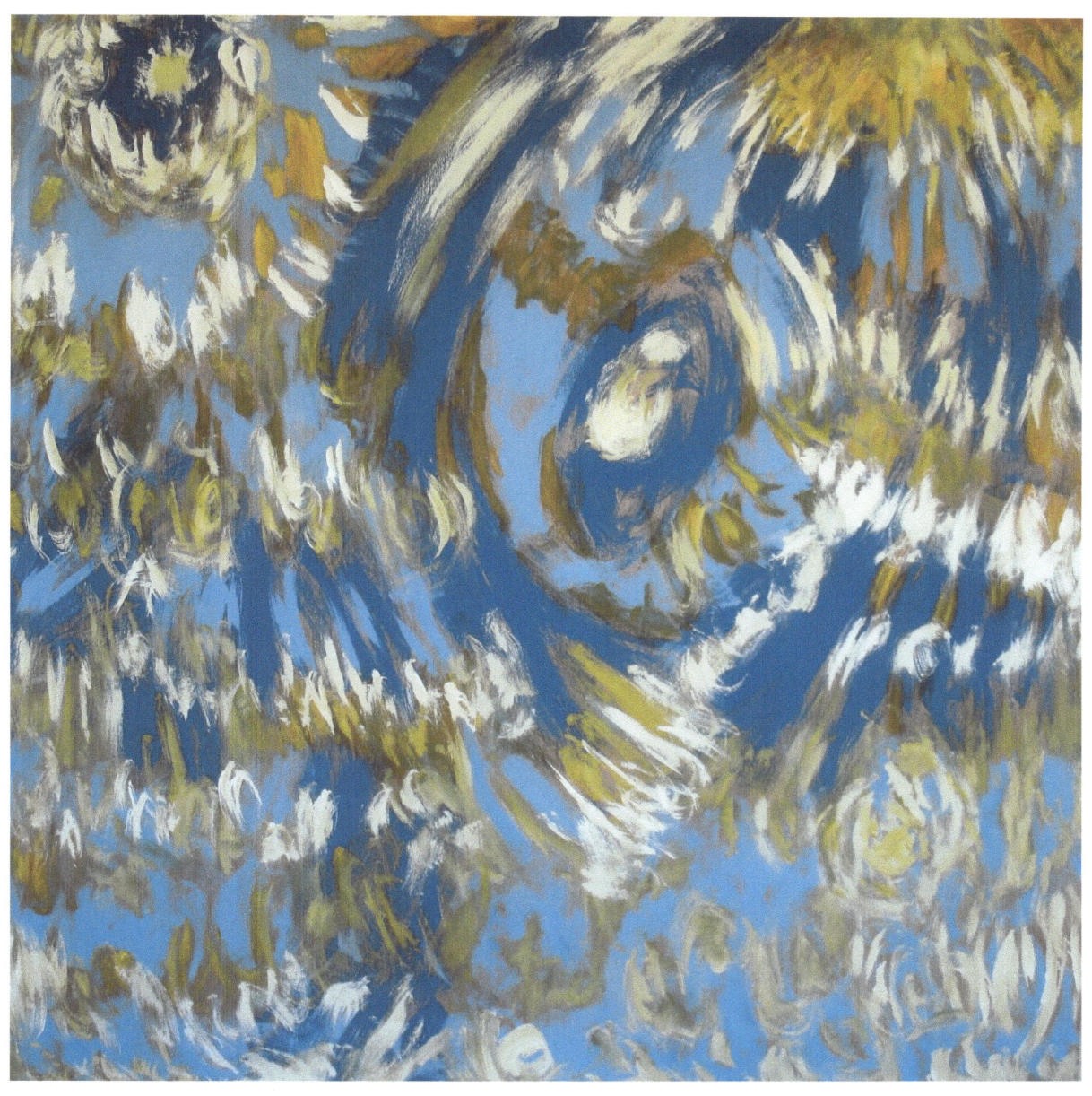

Summer Sky, 2010
Acrylic on wood panel
48 x 48 inches

jeffcase.com

Copyright 2020   All rights reserved   Jeff Allen Case

www.ingramcontent.com/pod-product-compliance
Lightning Source LLC
Chambersburg PA
CBHW051209220526
45473CB00003B/959